Good Lookin' Cookin'

With The Rodeo Grandmas

Lorraine

Janis

Peg

Chloe

The Grandmas
& Their
Friends Serve
Up A Hearty
Helping of
Homespun
Recipes

Compiled by the Rodeo Grandmas
Edited by Annie Morrow
Cover and publicity photos by Molly Morrow, Molly Morrow Photography
Designed By Zane Kinney

ISBN 0-9639167-8-5

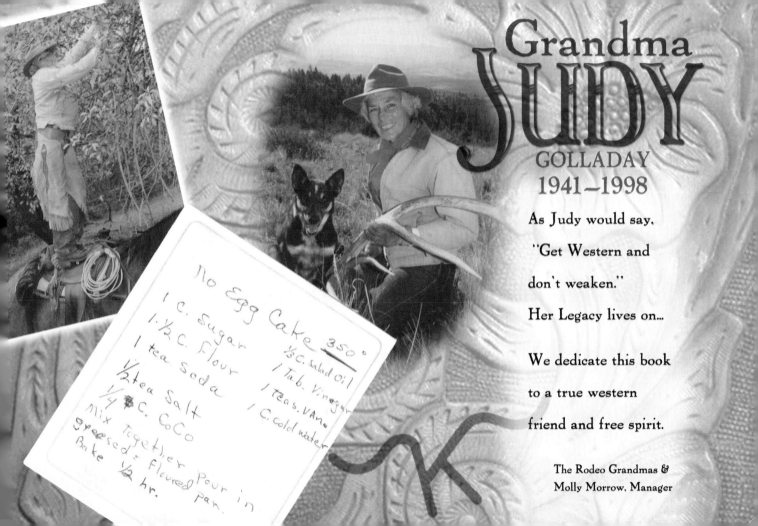

Grandma JUDY
GOLLADAY
1941–1998

As Judy would say,

"Get Western and

don't weaken."

Her Legacy lives on...

We dedicate this book

to a true western

friend and free spirit.

The Rodeo Grandmas &
Molly Morrow, Manager

No Egg Cake 350°
1 C. Sugar   ⅓ C. Salad Oil
1 ½ C. Flour   1 Tab. Vinegar
1 tea. Soda   1 Teas. Vanno
½ tea Salt   1 C. cold water
¼ C. CoCo
Mix Together Pour in
greased & Floured Pan.
Bake ½ hr.

The Rodeo Grandmas got their start when they were chosen to star in a commercial for Washington Mutual Bank. The 30-second television spot, later ads and their ability to please audiences with their true western grit brought these range-riding grandmothers instant fame. Since the commercials aired, the grandmas have made public appearances and have appeared on television programs such as "The Rosie O'Donnell Show", "CBS News This Morning", "Entertainment Tonight" and the most recently NBC's "Today" show. The Grandmas also have been guests of radio programs and featured in national and international newspapers and magazines.

The four Ellensburg women chosen for the commercial were Lorraine Plass, Peggy Minor Hunt, Janis Anderson, and Judy Golladay. They were hand-picked from a group of 20 Ellensburg cattlewomen who auditioned for the commercial. According to friends of the women, they were chosen because they capture the true western spirit.

Chloe Weidenbach joined The Rodeo Grandmas after Judy Golladay passed away in August of 1998.

For those believing that grandmothers who ride the range are out of the ordinary, the women would quickly remind you that people their age are still active. "A lot of people are old at 50," 73-year-old Peggy Hunt says, "But you have to keep busy every day and have something to get up for."

Each Rodeo Grandma has been riding since she was a child. Now they are all grandmothers and still riding the range in Washington state. These two facts taken together make for very interesting stories.

FEB. 10. 14

Oh! oh! shame on you

Grandma LORRAINE

AINT 'AT SOMPIN

LORRAINE

The eldest of The Rodeo Grandmas at 88, Lorraine Plass is also the most prolific with nine grandchildren and 19 great-grandchildren. Lorraine was born in Omaha, Nebraska and moved to a ranch in the Colorado Mountains when she was 9. She met her husband, George, at the National Western Stock Show and for the next 45 years, they boarded, broke, an trained horses, as well as taught riding on their ranch. After George retired in 1975, the couple moved to Washington to help their daughter Chloe and her husband, Eldon, on their Ellensburg ranch. A widow, after 63 years of marriage, Lorraine's not as active as she once was, but she still herds cattle each summer with Chloe and Eldon. Lorraine's ability to tell stories and yodel captivate many a listener.

2

JILL'S PARTY MIX

From my dear friend Jill McDowell who got this from her mother Neva Conner 40 years ago.

Mix together in a large turkey roaster pan:

4 cups Rice Chex

4 cups Corn Chex

4 cups Crispex

4 cups small stick pretzels

1 large can mixed nuts

½ large can cashews

½ large can pecans

Melt together:

¾ lb. butter

2 ½ Tblsp. Worcestshire Sauce

2¼ tsp. celery salt

1 tsp. garlic salt

¼ tsp. garlic powder

2 ½ tsp. seasoning salt

Spoon over dry mixture and stir

Bake at 250° for one hour, stirring every 10 minutes. Mixture can be left in a warm oven for several hours or overnight for added flavor. Bag up portions that are not used right away and freeze. Great when put in cannisters for Christmas gifts.

3

CREAM OF POTATO SOUP

4 medium size potatoes

½ medium onion

1 quart milk

2 Tbsp. flour

1 tsp. salt

pepper to taste

Cook potatoes until soft and run through a sieve. Mix with other ingredients. Dish up and enjoy.

DUMPLING RECIPE FOR STEW OR CHICKEN

1 cup flour

½ cup milk

1 egg

½ tsp. salt

2 tsp. baking powder

Break egg into bowl, then beat slightly and add milk. Into this, sift the dry ingredients. Add more milk if necessary to make a stiff dough. Drop by spoonfuls into stew & cover for about 20 minutes.

Remember when Oleo was white like lard and you were given a capsule of yellow food coloring to color it if you wanted?

GOLDEN MEAT LOAF

2 large apples

1 lb. ground beef

½ cup bread crumbs

1 small onion

1 egg, beaten

2 slices of bacon

1 tsp. salt

¼ tsp. pepper

¼ tsp. allspice

¼ tsp. dry mustard

Grate apples into large bowl. Add remaining ingredients and mix well. Pack into loaf pan. Top with bacon strips – bake 45 minutes at 375°. Garnish with apple slices.

SWEET AND SOUR PORK

1½ lbs. lean pork strips

½ cup water

1 can pineapple chunks

¼ cup brown sugar

1 Tbsp. cornstarch

¼ cup vinegar

3 Tbsp. soy sauce

1 small green pepper, cut in strips

1 small onion, sliced

½ cup celery

Brown pork, add water and simmer one hour. Drain pineapple. Combine juice, sugar, cornstarch, vinegar & soy sauce. Add to pork and stir until thick. Add pineapple, pepper, onion & celery. Cook 3 to 4 minutes. Serve over rice.

CHICKEN AND BISCUITS

½ cup chopped onion

2 Tbsp. butter

8 oz. cream cheese

1 can cream of mushroom soup

1¼ cup boned, cooked chicken

small can sliced mushrooms

2 Tbsp. sherry

pepper & salt to taste

Sauté onions in butter, blend in cream cheese. Add soup, pepper, chicken & mushrooms with liquid. Heat to boiling point and add sherry. Serve over biscuits.

CHICKEN AND ELBOW-RONI

2 cups cooked Elbow-Roni

2 cups grated American cheddar cheese

1½ cups cooked-up chicken

1 cup sliced canned mushrooms

1 can cream of chicken soup plus enough milk to make 2 cups

Mix ingredients, pour into buttered baking dish (2 quart). Bake 60 minutes. Makes 6 to 8 servings.

KRAUT POT PIE

1 lbs. sauerkraut

1 small onion

2 lbs. beef or ham

1 30-oz. can tomatoes

Place meat in pan. Cover with kraut, tomatoes, onion. Salt & pepper to taste and bake till done.

BEEF & VEGETABLE CASSEROLE

- 1 layer raw hamburger
- 1 layer chopped onion
- 1 layer raw carrots
- 1 layer raw potatoes
- 1 can cream of chicken soup

Put in casserole and pour soup over the top. Cover and bake at 350° for about 1 hour. Uncover and bake for 15 minutes.

"Any recipe is good for me!...I love 'em all, even the ones that don't taste good."

BEEF NOODLE BAKE

- 2 cups noodles
- 1 lb. ground beef
- 1½ cup chopped onion
- 2 cups chopped celery
- 1 can tomato soup
- 3 Tbsp. chopped green pepper
- 1 Tbsp. shortening
- 1 tsp. salt
- 1 tsp. soy sauce

Cook noodles until tender, drain. Cook meat, celery, pepper until meat is brown. Add salt, soy sauce & tomato soup. Bring to boil. Combine noodles with ½ meat mixture & pour into casserole. Top with remaining meat mixture. Bake at 350° for 30 minutes.

7

LASAGNA PRESTO

½ lbs. ground beef

1 chopped onion

2 cloves garlic

2 tsp. oregano

½ cup water

2 tsp. vinegar

½ lb. lasagna noodles - cooked

2 cans tomato soup

1 pint cottage cheese

½ lb. mozzarella cheese sliced

Brown beef and add onion, garlic & oregano. Add soup, water, vinegar and simmer for 30 minutes, stirring occasionally. In a lightly greased 12x8x2 baking dish arrange three alternating layers of noodles, cottage cheese, meat sauce & mozzarella. Top with parmesan cheese. Bake in 350° oven 30 minutes. Let stand for 30 minutes before cutting into squares.

BAKED SALMON

salmon fillet(s)

1 ½ cup yogurt or mayonaise

2 tsp. crushed garlic

½ tsp. tarragon

1 tsp. dill

1tsp. salt

pepper

Mix the yogurt/mayonaise with garlic, salt and herbs. Spread on the flesh side of the salmon and place skin side down on a broiler pan and broil under moderate heat. This one is even better on a barbecue grill.

GRANDPA'S POKER BEANS

Thank you to Mike Mahaffey, "A Rodeo Grandma Roadie", for this great recipe!

1 lb. Polish sausage sliced like poker chips

½ lb. bacon, sliced

1 med. onion, diced

¼ cup ketchup

¼ cup yellow mustard

¼ cup vinegar

¾ cup brown sugar

4 oz. can diced green chilies

large can pork and beans (undrained)

reg. can navy beans (drained)

reg. can kidney beans (drained)

reg. can large butter beans (drained)

dash of garlic powder

Brown bacon, sausage, green chilies and onion until onions are clear and soft. Drain as much fat as you like. Add ketchup, mustard, vinegar, garlic powder and brown sugar. Mix thoroughly and let things cook together for a minute or two. Take a minute to enjoy the wonderful aroma here. Add the beans (pork and beans first), stir well, cover and let simmer for 10 minutes at a low heat. Taste frequently to make sure all is well. If it tastes wrong, add a little right.

You can add or substitute black beans, chili beans, black-eyed peas, great Northern beans, pintos or any other you like. You can zip them up with chili powder, cayenne or jalapenos.

9

APPLE NUT CAKE

1 cup sugar

⅓ cup shortening

2 eggs beaten

2 cups apples cut fine

1¼ cup flour

½ tsp cinnamon

½ tsp soda

½ tsp baking powder

½ tsp salt

½ cup nuts

1 tsp vanilla

Stir ingredients together – put in 8x8 pan. Bake 350° to 45 minutes.

APPLE CRISP

4 cups apples

⅔ cup brown sugar

½ cup flour

½ cup oatmeal

¾ tsp. cinnamon

¾ tsp. nutmeg

⅓ cup margarine

Grease 8x8 pan. Fill bottom with sliced apples. Mix remaining ingredients and spread over apples. Bake for 30 minutes at 375°.

RHUBARB CRISP

- 4 rhubarb stalks, chopped
- ¾ cup flour
- 1½ cups sugar, half brown & half white
- 1 tsp. cinnamon
- ½ cup butter

Place rhubarb in greased 8-inch pan. Mix dry ingredients & spoon over rhubarb. Bake at 350° for 45 minutes. Serve topped with whipped cream if desired.

PIE CRUST

Thank you to our dear Dorie Mahaffey.

- 1 cup flour... it is critical to use blended soft & hard wheat flour
- 6 heaping Tbsp. yellow shortening
- sprinkle of salt
- 3 Tbsp. cold water

Cut shortening into flour and salt, sprinkle with cold water and toss gently with a fork to moisten. Do not overmix. Gather into a ball and turn out onto a lightly floured board, kneading gently if necessary. Flatten gently with your hand and roll out into a ³⁄₁₆ inch circle and fit into pie plate...the less handling the better...

Leaf lard (the large pieces of fat as it was trimmed off the carcass) was given to you at the butcher shop. We cut it into pieces and rendered it to make lard.

11

IMPOSSIBLE PIE

2 cups milk

¾ cup sugar

4 eggs   1 cup coconut

½ tsp. salt   ¼ cup flour

1 tsp. vanilla

Blend and place in greased pie tin. Bake at 350° for 45 minutes.

PLAIN MUFFINS

2 cups flour

4 Tbsp. sugar

2 Tbsp. shortening

4 tsp. baking powder

½ tsp. salt

1 egg

1 cup milk

Add baking powder, salt, egg and milk to dry ingredients. Fill muffin tins ⅔ full. Bake in 400° oven for 25 minutes.

CORN CAKES

1½ cups flour

1 cup corn meal

4 tsp. baking powder

1½ cups boiling water

¼ cup milk

1 egg

1½ tsp. salt

2 Tbsp. shortening

¼ cup sugar

Add cornmeal to boiling water and boil five minutes. Place in bowl and add milk and dry ingredients. Stir in egg and shortening. Cook the same as you would "hot cakes."

12

TRADITIONAL ENGLISH COOKIE

1 cup soft butter (2 cubes)

½ cup sugar

1 egg

3 tsp. vanilla

3 cups flour

½ tsp. baking powder

Mix butter, sugar, & egg. Stir in vanilla and then chill dough. Roll lightly on floured board and cut into shapes. Bake until lightly brown at 425° for 5 to 7 minutes. Makes six dozen cookies.

PEANUT BUTTER LOGS

1 cup peanut butter

¼ cup margarine or butter

1½ cup confectioner sugar

3 cups oven toasted rice cereal

1 cup chopped nuts

1 6-oz. pkg. semi-sweet chocolate

2 Tbsp. shortening

Beat together peanut butter & margarine. Stir in cereal and then portion dough in teaspoonfuls. Shape into logs & roll in nuts. Heat chocolate & shortening, drizzle over logs, and enjoy.

The cowboys always mixed their biscuits in the top of the flour sack...they made a little well, added all their ingredients, then mixed the dough and took it out and baked it.

OLD-FASHIONED RICE PUDDING

¼ cup rice

4 cups milk

¼ tsp. salt

⅓ cup sugar

½ tsp. vanilla

Mix ingredients and pour into buttered baking dishes. Bake 3 hours at 250°. Stir occasionally to keep rice from settling (until done).

Lorraine has two children, nine grandchildren, 18 great grandchildren, and one on the road.

MINCE MEAT

2 lbs. neck meat (beef or venison) cooked, boned and ground

5 lbs. apples peeled, seeded, and chopped

1 lb. raisins

2 lbs. currants

2½ lbs. brown sugar

1 quart boiled cider

1 pint brandy

1½ tsp. cinnamon

1 Tbsp. nutmeg

l Tbsp. cloves

2 Tbsp. salt

Mix all ingredients together and can, freeze, or make into mince meat pie (see pie crust recipe).

14

SAUCES, SYRUPS & TOPPERS FOR YOUR TASTEBUDS

CREAM CHEESE SPREAD

2 Tbsp. brown sugar

1 3-oz. pkg. cream cheese

1 Tbsp. orange peel, grated

1 Tbsp. orange juice

Mix ingredients until smooth. Refrigerate until needed.

On a daily basis, I mix 1 teaspoon of honey and 2 teaspoons vinegar in a small glass of warm water and drink...it'll either cure ya or kill ya...and I'm still alive.

15

LIQUEURS, CORDIALS & OTHER SIPPIN' STUFF

CHERRY CORDIAL

From our dear one, Dorie Mahaffey, Molly's mom.

Fill a gallon jar with fresh cherries. Add l cup sugar and a fifth of vodka. Let sit for l0 days, mixing daily by rocking jar back and forth several times. Strain and sip the juice as a liqueur. The cherries can be eaten and they are very good over ice cream. You also can substitute other fresh berries.

HOMEMADE KAHLUA
Coffee-flavored liqueur
Thank you, Jill McDowell

- 3½ cup sugar
- 2 cup water
- 1 whole vanilla bean - chopped (you can get these at the health food store)
- 2 oz. instant coffee (14 tbsp.)
- 2 cup boiling water
- 1 quart vodka

In a small sauce pan, combine sugar, vanilla bean, and tap water. Place over moderate heat and stir until sugar is dissolved. Continue cooking on low heat for 30 minutes without stirring.

Meanwhile, in a large bowl mix coffee with boiling water. Stir in vodka, strain vanilla syrup into vodka mixture.

Mix well and pour into sterilzed bottles. Cap or cork bottles. Must age for at least 30 days.

IN A HURRY, LET'S DO IT THE EASY WAY

SPAGHETTI PIZZA

8 oz. spaghetti noodles

mozzarella cheese, grated

pepperoni

pizza sauce

onion

green pepper

black olives, sliced

Cook spaghetti, mix in half of sauce, put in bottom of 9x13 greased pan. Spread other ½ of sauce over spaghetti. Layer in order: pepperoni, onion, green pepper, olives, and mozzarella cheese. Bake 25-30 min in 350° oven. Let stand 10 minutes before cutting.

TUNA FISH OPEN-FACERS

2–7-oz. cans tuna fish, drained & flaked

⅓ cup chopped celery

1 hard cooked egg - cut into small pieces

1 cup (4 oz) shredded cheddar cheese

½ tsp. prepared mustard

2 Tbsp. mayonnaise

1 can (8 oz) refrigerator biscuits

Combine tuna, celery, egg & ½ cup of cheese. Combine mustard & mayonnaise and add mixture to tuna. Mix lightly but thoroughly. If necessary, add more mayonnaise to hold mixture together. Separate biscuit dough into 10 biscuits. Pat out each biscuit into 4 inch circle. Spoon about ¼ cups tuna mixture on each biscuit. Sprinkle remaining cheese over each - place on greased baking sheet - place in 400° oven for 10 or 15 minutes until brown. Makes 10 open face sandwiches.

17

SLOPPY JOES

   1 lb. ground beef

   1 pkg. sloppy joe seasoning

   1 6-oz. can tomato paste

   ¼ can water

   Hamburger buns

Brown beef in skillet. Add seasoning, tomato paste and water. Heat to boiling and simmer 10 minutes. Stir. Pour over buns.

ONE DISH MEAL

Grandma Lorraine makes this one just to get out of the kitchen.

   1 lb. hamburger

   2 med. potatoes

   1 can green beans with juice

Put all ingredients in a pan or skillet and add onions or garlic with salt and pepper. Cook at a medium heat until potatoes and meat are done.

GOULASH

   1 box of macaroni as directed on box. Omit cheese.

   ½ to 1 lb. of hamburger, cooked

   1 6-oz. can tomato paste or sauce

Mix together.
You can use the cheese if desired.

My chairs were all wired for "strength", as the kids used them for "bucking horses".

18

Grandma
PEGGY

Peggy Hunt is a former rodeo star who got her start with a little cotton rope her father gave to her when she was 11. She replaced the cotton rope with a Samson Spot Cord, and took her increasing repertoire of tricks to horse shows and rodeos while still in high school. In 1947, Peggy bought a trick riding saddle from Monte Montana, and was then able to both trick ride and rope on her little bay horse, Pepper. Together, Peggy and Pepper worked rodeos throughout the Northwest and Canada. Today at 73, Peggy can be found riding her horse, T.Q. on her 62-acre ranch in the Reecer Creek area and spending time with her nine grandchildren.

DIPS, MIXES & OTHER STUFF FOR GRAZIN'

SEVEN LAYER BEAN DIP

Thanks to my daughter, Kris Olson, for this one.

- 1 can refried beans
- chili powder to taste
- ½ pint sour cream
- 1 package guacamole/avacado dip
- 1 can sliced olives
- 8 oz. cheddar cheese, shredded
- 1 package taco seasoning
- 1 large tomato (sliced & cut into cubes)

Mix refried beans with chili powder. Layer bottom of pan with beans, then guacamole, follow with mixture of sour cream and taco seasoning, top with cheese, tomatoes, and olives. (green onions optional.)

FRUITS, VEGGIES & OTHER RANGE SALADS

ICE BOX PICKLES

My thanks to Evelyn Carlson

- water
- 7 cups cucumbers
- 1 cup onion
- 1 green pepper
- 1 Tbsp. pickling spice
- 2 cups sugar
- 1 cup white vinegar
- 1 Tbsp. celery seed

Slice cucumbers and mix with onion, green pepper and pickling spice in water. Let stand for one hour. Drain. Bring to boil sugar, vinegar and celery seed. Pour over cucumber mixture and refrigerate. Three batches will fill a gallon jar. Use as needed.

21

FRUIT SALAD

Thanks to my sister, B.J. Reichert.

- **1 small pkg. vanilla instant pudding**
- **½ can of 6 oz. orange juice, frozen**
- **1 cup milk**
- **12 oz. whipped topping**
- **pineapple**
- **bananas**
- **grapes**
- **cantaloupe**
- **strawberries**

Mix pudding, orange juice and milk and let set until thick. Stir cool whip into vanilla mix. Layer fruit with dressing between each layer. Refreshing summer fruit salad!

YUMMY SALAD

Thank you to my daughter Sheri Wippel.

- **1 box cream cheese**
- **about 30 marshmallows**
- **1 can evaporated milk**
- **1 medium size tub of wipped topping**
- **1 can crushed pineapple**
- **graham crackers**

On low heat melt cream cheese, marshmallows and milk, but do not scorch. Pour into bowl or pan to cool in refrigerator, but do not allow mixture to set into a mold yet. When cool, mix in pineapple and Cool Whip. Put salad in mold, if desired, and let set. To garnish, sprinkle with crushed graham crackers.

CUCUMBERS IN SOUR CREAM

Thank you Lucille Johnson.

- 2 cucumbers, sliced
- 1 large onion, sliced and separated into rings
- 1 pint sour cream (may use imitation)
- 1 Tbsp. vinegar
- 2 Tbsp. lemon juice
- ¾ cup sugar

Beat sugar, vinegar, lemon juice and sour cream until smooth. Slice cucumbers and onions. Stir into sour cream mixture. Chill.

SOUPS, CHILIES & OTHER POTS ON THE FIRE

HAMBURGER STEW

- 3½ cup diced potatoes
- 1 (No. 2) can kidney beans
- 1 large onion, diced
- 2 Tbsp. butter
- 1 lb. ground beef
- 1 can tomatoes
- ¾ cup ketchup
- salt and pepper to taste

Boil potatoes and add beans. Place butter in large skillet and brown onion and beef. Add tomatoes, ketchup, salt and pepper. Cook for five minutes, then add potatoes and beans. Cover and cook for 10 minutes.

MEATS, CASSEROLES & OTHER COWPOKE VITTLES

SALMON LOAF

1 cup cooked salmon

1 cup bread crumbs

1 cup scalded milk

1 tsp. salt

1 Tbsp. butter

1 tsp. onion bits

1 tsp. lemon juice

2 egg yolks (beaten)

2 egg whites (beaten)

Pour scalded milk over bread crumbs. Add all other ingredients except egg whites. Mix, then add egg whites. Pour into well-greased loaf pan and bake one hour at 350°.

VEGETABLE LOAF

This all-vegetable dish tastes like meat loaf. Thank you to my friend, Lucille Johnson.

2 cups grated carrots

2 cups minced celery

1 small onion

parsley

½ cup ground nuts

4 Tbsp. melted butter

1 cup bread crumbs

1 egg

Mix ingredients and place in greased loaf pan. Bake one hour at 350°. Serve with mushroom sauce, such as cream of mushroom soup.

HAMBURGER CORN BAKE

Thank you to Mickey Thayer for this great recipe!

- 1½ lb. ground beef
- 1 cup chopped onions
- 1 12-oz. can whole kernel corn
- 1 10-oz. can cream of chicken soup
- 1 10-oz. Can cream of mushroom soup
- 1 cup dairy sour cream
- l cup chopped pimiento
- ¾ tsp. salt   ½ tsp. pepper
- 6 oz. (3 cups) medium noodles, cooked and drained
- 1 cup soft bread crumbs
- 2 Tbsp. butter or margarine

Brown hamburger, drain off fat. Add onions and cook until tender. Add all ingredients except bread crumbs and butter or margarine. Put into 2-qt. casserole dish. Combine bread crumbs and butter or margarine, sprinkle on top. Bake at 350° for 45 minutes.

STROGANOFF

This is Jim Olson's great recipe.

- 1 lb. ground meat
- 1 med. onion
- 1 can cream of mushroom soup
- 1 cup milk
- sour cream to taste
- 1 pkg. egg noodles

Brown hamburger, onion and mushrooms. Drain. Cook noodles. Add sour cream to hamburger mixture, mix in noodles and season to taste. Serves 2 to 4.

25

CHELSY'S LAZY DAY LASAGNA

Thank you to my darling granddaughter, Chelsy, for this one.

- **1lb. hamburger**
- **oregano**
- **6 oz. lasagna noodles**
- **15 oz. spaghetti sauce**
- **8 oz. cottage cheese**
- **6 oz. mozzarella cheese**

Fry hamburger, then add oregano and sauce. Cook noodles and drain. In greased baking dish, layer half each of: noodles, cottage cheese, mozzarella cheese, and sauce mixture. Repeat. Bake at 375° for 30 minutes.

Every other day I drink a small glass of orange juice mixed with one teaspoon of cod liver oil and one tablespoon of brewers yeast along with my daily vitamins.

TWICE-BAKED POTATOES

Thanks to my daughter, Kris.

4 large potatoes

⅓ to ½ cup milk

¼ cup margarine or butter

¼ cup sour cream

½ tsp. salt

dash of pepper

grated cheese

Prepare and bake four large potatoes at 375° for 1–1½ hours. Poke holes with fork and rub with margarine. Increase oven temperature after removing potatoes to 400°. Cut a thin slice from top of each potato, scoop out inside, leaving a thin shell. Mash potatoes until no lumps remain. Add milk in small amounts, beating after each addition (amount of milk varies). Add margarine or butter, sour cream, salt, and pepper. Beat until potatoes are light and fluffy. Fill shells, then bake for 15 minutes. Sprinkle with cheese and bake five more minutes.

27

CHEESY POTATO BAKE

Thanks to Sally Dunlop.

- one 2-lb. bag frozen cubed hash browns
- 1 can cream of chicken soup
- 1 pt. sour cream
- four 6-oz. jars cheese whiz
- 2 cups grated cheddar cheese
- 2 Tbsp. onion flakes
- 1 cup potato chip crumbs
- sliced almonds

Put hash browns in 9x13 pan and let thaw ½ hour. Pour melted butter over top. Mix soup, cheese whiz, onion, cheddar cheese and sour cream. Pour over potatoes and mix. After ½ hour top with potato chip crumbs and almonds and butter. Salt and pepper to taste. Bake at 350° for one hour.

28

BREADS, DESSERTS & OTHER SWEETS FROM THE RANGE

HOLIDAY CARROT PUDDING

My thanks to l04-year-old Mable Abrahamson, a grandmother and horsewoman like me.

As tradition has it, Mable's granddaughter, Connie Bennett took Rodeo Grandma Judy's job after she passed away as "the range rider" for the Bar Balloon Ranch. The Bar Balloon Ranch holds, and currently uses, the oldest registered brand in the state of Washington.

Sift together:

1½ cups flour	⅓ cup sugar
1 tsp. salt	1 tsp. soda

Continued…

Add:

- 1½ cups grated carrots
- 1½ cups raw apples-chopped fine
- 1 cup raisins or chopped dates or figs
- ½ cup suet or butter
- ¼ cup light molasses
- 1 cup chopped nuts

Mix gently. Put mixture into a generously greased pudding mold or 1 pound coffee can. Fill to ½ to ¾ full and steam for 2½ hours. A commercial steamer, a deep well cooker with a wire frame, or a deep kettle that holds enough water to last through the entire cooking time may be used. Canning jar rings may be used as stilts to keep pudding vessel from resting on the bottom of the kettle. Also, tie wax paper around the mold to prevent water from dripping on the top of the pudding. When the pudding is done, remove from the steamer and remove the wax paper from the top of the mold. Loosen pudding from the mold by laying the vessel on its side to let air in and turn out to a warm serving dish. Serve warm with Hard Sauce.

HARD SAUCE

Combine:

- 1 cup cream or canned milk
- 1 cup sugar
- ½ cup butter

Bring to a boil, then drizzle over warm pudding and serve. Pudding may be kept warm for later serving, but drizzle hard sauce just before serving.

FLAMING PRESENTATION

Pour a small amount of brandy over pudding and light. You can also soak lumps of sugar in orange or lemon extract, place around pudding base and light.

29

POTATO ROLLS

Thanks to my friend, Joyce Weekes.

2 cups warm water

$\frac{1}{3}$ **cup sugar**   **2 tsp. salt**

2 pkg. rapid rise yeast

2 cups flour

$\frac{1}{2}$ **cup potato flakes or buds**

2 eggs $\frac{1}{3}$ **cup oil**

3 $\frac{1}{2}$ to 4 cups flour

Mix very well with hand mixer.

Then add:

Mix water, sugar and yeast in large bowl to soften yeast. Then add salt, potato flakes, eggs, oil and 2 cups flour. Mix very well with hand mixer. Finally, add 3½ to 4 cups flour to make a soft dough. Form into a ball and put in a second bowl that is greased. Let rise for 1 hour or more. Then roll dough out about 2 inches thick onto floured board and cut with biscuit cutter into rolls. Let rise on cookie sheets for $\frac{1}{2}$ hour or more. Bake at 400° degrees for 10-12 minutes.

TEXAS SHEET CAKE

This Texas-sized cake from my friend, Lucille.

2 cups flour   **2 cups sugar**

4 and $\frac{1}{2}$ Tbsp. cocoa

1 tsp. salt   **1 cube butter**

$\frac{1}{2}$ **cup shortening**

1 cup water   **2 eggs**

1 tsp. baking soda

almost $\frac{1}{2}$ cup milk

1 tsp. vinegar

Mix together flour, sugar, cocoa and salt. Bring to boil butter, shortening and water. Stir all ingredients together and then add eggs. Combine soda, milk and vinegar to make buttermilk. Add to batter and beat one minute. Bake batter in greased and floured pan. If using a pan similar to a jelly roll pan, bake at 350° for 30-40 minutes. Bake at 325° if using a glass pan. Serves 20.

Continued…

Frosting:

- 1 stick margarine
- 6 Tblsp. milk
- 1 tsp. vanilla
- 4 Tblsp. cocoa
- 1 box powdered sugar
- ½ cup chopped nuts (optional)

Mix margarine, milk and cocoa and bring to a boil. Remove from heat and add powdered sugar and vanilla. Mix in nuts if desired. Let frosting stand for 3-4 minutes, then spread on cake while frosting is warm.

Baking Christmas goodies was always fun with my daughters—"bumping" around in the kitchen together.

APPLE CRISP

We all loved it when Grandma Alice Hunt would make this.

- 4 cups sliced apples
- 1 tsp. cinnamon
- 1 tsp. salt
- ¼ cup water
- ¾ cup sifted flour
- 1 cup sugar
- ⅓ cup butter

Place apples in buttered baking dish, sprinkle with cinnamon, salt and water. Mix together flour, sugar and butter. Drop this over the apples. Bake 40 minutes at 350° and serve warm with cream.

31

COWBOY CAKE

This recipe was given to my friend, Joyce, by her husband, Martin Weekes. It had been passed down from his mother.

> 5 eggs
>
> 2 Tbsp. flour
>
> 1 qt. milk
>
> butter
>
> sugar
>
> cinnamon and/or nutmeg

Beat eggs well, blend in flour, then add milk and beat. Bake in glass baking pan, 9" x 12" or smaller if you like a thicker cake, at 350° until knife inserted pulls out clean. Add other ingredients while warm. Flavor to each individual's taste.

CRAZY CAKE

This is my favorite cake. So quick and delicious, I love to mix it up.

> 1 cup oil
>
> 2 cup sugar
>
> 2 cup water
>
> 2 tsp. vinegar
>
> 2 tsp. vanilla
>
> 3 cup flour
>
> 1 tsp. salt
>
> 1 tsp. soda
>
> 1 tsp. baking powder
>
> ⅓ cup cocoa

Mix ingredients, then place in an oblong pan. Bake at 350° for 50 minutes.

For brandings, birthdays and gatherings, I made Crazy Cake. It was a favorite and very easy to make. I also would cook a big pot roast with potatoes, carrots and onions. I also made cinnamon rolls.

MOM'S ICING OR FUDGE

My friend Joyce received this recipe from her mother, Mrs. Jack Guyer of North Dakota.

1 cup cream

2 cup sugar

½ scant cup cocoa (optional)

2 Tbsp. butter

1 tsp. vanilla

If you choose to make chocolate, mix the cocoa with sugar, then add the cream and cook on medium heat in a 2 quart pot. Cook until it boils (for a couple of minutes) stirring occasionally (don't over stir or it sugars.) Then check: a soft ball will form when a teaspoon of icing is placed in a cup of ice cold water. Add vanilla and butter. Put pot filled with cooked icing in a sink of cold water to cool. Whip until creamy and ice your cake. You can use the same recipe for fudge, except bring to a hard ball stage.

CHOCOLATE CHIP PIE

½ cup white sugar

½ cup flour

½ cup brown sugar

2 cups milk

3 eggs, separated

1tsp. vanilla

6 oz. chocolate chips

Mix dry ingredients with milk and heat in a saucepan until thick (about 15 minutes.) Add egg yolks and cook for five minutes. Stir in vanilla and chocolate chips, then pour in an already-baked pie crust. Chill. For a meringue top, beat egg whites and some sugar, then spread over top of chilled pie. Place in broiler to brown.

33

PEGGY

PIE CRUST COOKIES

3 cups sifted flour

1 cup shortening

1 cup sugar

1 cup ground raisins

1 cup chopped nuts

1 tsp. salt

3 tbsp. sour cream

½ tsp. baking powder

1 tsp. soda

1 tsp. vanilla

Mix flour, shortening, sugar, raisins, nuts, and salt in order given and work as for pie crust. Work in the other ingredients. You can add chocolate or peanut butter to mix as desired. Bake at 375° for 12 to 15 minutes.

DREAM BARS

Thanks to my friend Alice Jensen.

Crust:

½ cup butter

½ cup brown sugar

1 cup flour

Topping:

1 cup brown sugar

2 eggs

2 Tbsp. flour

½ tsp. baking powder

¼ tsp. salt

½ tsp. vanilla

1½ cups coconuts

1 cup nuts

Cream butter, sugar and flour. Place the mixture in an 8x12 pan and bake 10 minutes. Mix topping ingredients and spread over crust. Bake 20 minutes.

34

LACEY'S MONSTER COOKIES

My granddaughter Lacey provided me with these "monstrous" treats.

1 lb. brown sugar

½ lb. butter

2 cup sugar

¼ cup corn syrup

6 eggs

1½ lbs. peanut butter

9 cup oatmeal

4 tsp. baking soda

½ lb. chocolate chips

½ lb. M&M's

1½ Tblsp. vanilla

Mix ingredients and drop spoonfuls on a cookie sheet. Bake at 350° for 12 minutes.

CHOCO-MARSHMALLOW COOKIES

1¾ cup sifted flour

½ tsp. salt　　　　**½ tsp. soda**

½ cup cocoa

½ cup shortening　　**1 cup sugar**

1 egg

¼ cup milk　　　　**1 tsp. vanilla**

18 marshmallows cut in half

one-half cup pecans (optional)

Sift together flour, salt, soda, and cocoa. Cream shortening and sugar, add egg, vanilla and milk, beating well. Add dry ingredients and mix. Drop by teaspoon-fulls onto greased baking sheet.

Bake in oven at 350 for eight minutes. Do not overbake. Remove from oven and press marshmallows, cut side down, on top of each cookie. Bake for two minutes longer. Remove from oven, cool and top with cocoa frosting and pecan half.

35

SAUCES, SYRUPS & OTHER TOPPERS FOR YOUR TASTEBUDS

COCOA FROSTING

Thanks to my friend Alice Jensen.

2 cups confectioner's sugar

5 Tbsp. cocoa

⅛ tsp. Salt

3 Tbsp. soft butter or margarine

4-5 Tbsp. light cream or milk

Combine confectioner's sugar, cocoa and salt. Add butter or margarine and light cream or milk.

IN A HURRY, LET'S DO IT THE EASY WAY

CHOCOLATE FUDGE COOKIES

Thank you, Alice.

⅓ cup milk

3 Tbsp. cocoa

¼ lb. margarine

dash of salt

½ cup peanut butter

2¾ cup rolled oats

vanilla

Boil milk, cocoa, margarine and salt for one minute. Add peanut butter, oats and vanilla and mix thoroughly. Drop on wax paper and let dry.

MUD PIE

This is a favorite of Martha Smith and mine.

30 Oreo cookies

¼ **cup margarine, melted**

½ **gallon vanilla ice cream**

Fudge topping

1 small tub whipped topping

Crush cookies and save ⅓ for top. Mix margarine with cookies. Layer the cookies on the bottom, then ice cream, fudge, Cool Whip, then extra cookies. Freeze and enjoy.

Peg has four children and nine grandchildren.

CINNAMON APPLE TOAST

This one is a favorite when it is too late to make a pie—but you know your not going to sleep before you satisfy that sweet tooth.

1 or 2 slices of bread per person

sliced apples

butter or margerine

cinnamon

sugar

Butter the bread (day old works better). Lay sliced apples on top, then sprinkle cinnamon and sugar on top. Place on a baking sheet and bake at 350° until apples are soft and cinnamon and sugar begins to brown, about 10–15 minutes.

37

SIX CUP FRUIT SALAD

Thanks, Charlene Stone.

- **1 cup sour cream**
- **1 cup mandarin oranges**
- **1 cup small marshmallows**
- **1 cup pineapple**
- **1 cup coconut**
- **1 cup grapes**

Mix together and enjoy.

BROCCOLI CASSEROLE

Thank you , B.J.

- **2 pkgs. frozen broccoli**
- **1 cup instant rice**
- **1 can cream of chicken soup**
- **one-half cup milk**
- **1 small jar cheese spread**

Cook broccoli until tender. Drain. Mix other ingredients and pour over broccoli. Put buttered bread crumbs over top and bake 45 minutes at 350°.

Every year I raised 50 chickens and dressed them for the freezer...I really enjoyed this. I also liked to garden and ride in the hills with my family to bring out the cattle.

Grandma JANIS

going to town with her spurs on!

C-6042

Born into a ranching family in Northern California, Janis Capezzoli Anderson and her sister, Joanne, grew up helping their parents with ranch work which included everything from gathering, driving, and branding cattle, to putting up crops and raising sheep. Marriage brought Janis to Central Washington where she ranches with her husband Jerry. One winter, Janis and Jerry took the night shift to help their family in calving out 160 heifers. At 64, Janis rides and ropes with her family, including her three grandsons. She achieved a goal in 2000, winning second place out of 200 teams at a Cave Creek Team Roping Jackpot, in Arizona. All the grandkids say, "Go Granny Go!"

DIPS, MIXES & OTHER STUFF FOR GRAZIN'

JALAPENO TORTILLA ROLLS

12 oz. whipped cream cheese

3 Tbsp. chopped jalapenos

3 Tbsp. chopped pecans

3 Tbsp. chopped olives

5 Tbsp. chopped green onions

sprinkle of garlic powder

flour tortillas

Combine all ingredients and spread on tortillas. Roll up, refrigerate and slice one inch thick when ready to serve.

GUACAMOLE DIP

2 large, very ripe avocados

2 Tbsp. minced onion

2 Tbsp. mayonnaise

2 Tbsp. lemon juice

2 tsp. paprika

2 tsp. salt

½ tsp. Worcestershire sauce

3 to 4 drops hot pepper sauce

Mix ingredients together. Very tasty with chips!

FAVORITE SAYING: Let's go rope.

41

FRUITS, VEGGIES & OTHER RANGE SALADS

HAZEL'S CRANBERRY SALAD

In memory of my husband's mother, Hazel Anderson. This recipe continues to be enjoyed by the family.

3 cups cranberries, ground coarsely

1 cup sugar, add to berries and let sit while mixing jello

1 cup finely chopped celery

½ cup chopped nuts

1 package lemon jello

1 cup boiling water

Dissolve jello in boiling water and add 1 cup cold water. Add cranberry/sugar mixture, celery and nuts. Mold in serving bowl.

A HAPPY HOME RECIPE

4 cups love

2 cups loyalty

3 cups forgiveness

1 cup friendship

5 spoonfuls hope

2 cups tenderness

4 quarts faith

1 barrel of laughter

Take love and loyalty, mix thoroughly with faith. Blend with tenderness, kindness and understanding. Add friendship and hope, sprinkle abundantly with laughter. Bake all together with sunshine. Serve daily in generous helpings.

SOUTHWEST WHITE CHILI

I learned to make this chili in Arizona and it is
a big hit with the cowboys!

- 1 Tbsp. olive oil
- 1½ lb. boneless, skinless chicken breast,
  cut into small cubes
- ¼ cup chopped onion
- 1 cup chicken broth
- 1 4-oz. can of chopped green chilies
- 2 green onions, sliced
- 1 19-oz. can white kidney beans,
  undrained

Southwest spice blend:

- 1 tsp. garlic powder
- 1 tsp. ground red pepper
- 1 tsp. ground cumin
- ½ tsp. oregano leaves
- ½ tsp. cilantro (dried)

Heat oil in large saucepan over medium-high
heat, add chicken and onions, and cook 4-5
minutes. Stir in broth, green chilies, and
Southwest spice blend. Simmer for 15
minutes. Top with onions and garnish with
Monterey jack cheese, if desired.

43

TEXAS BEEF CHILI

This is a favorite recipe of my husband's family

6 dried Ancho/Pasilla chilies (very important to use this type of chilies for taste)

3½ cups boiling beef broth

3 lb. boneless beef chuck

2 Tbs. vegetable oil

1 large chopped onion

4 large garlic cloves, crushed and finely chopped

½ tsp. salt

2 tsp. ground cumin seed

1 to 3 Tbsp. chili powder

1 to 2 Tbls. cornmeal (optional)

Remove stem from chilies. Remove seeds, chop coarsely. Place chilies in bowl and cover with beef broth. Let steep for 30 minutes. Cut beef into ½ inch cubes. Heat oil in Dutch oven. Add onion. Cook, stirring constantly until soft and lightly browned. Add garlic, salt and beef. Cook, stirring constantly, just until beef looses its pink color. Strain chilies; reserve liquid and chilies. Stir 2½ cups of liquid from chilies into beef. Stir in chili powder and cumin seed. Heat to boiling; reduce heat and simmer over medium-low heat, uncovered for 1 hour. Stir occasionally during cooking. Place soaked chilies and remaining liquid in blender container, cover and blend until smooth. (If necessary, add about ½ cup water). stir into beef mixture. Cook over med/low heat 30 minutes or until tender.

Freeze extra vegetable cooking juices for later use in soups.

44

MEATS, CASSEROLES & OTHER COWPOKE VITTLES

CHICKEN CASSEROLE

Our family loves this casserole that my daughter, Mary, is always glad to make for us.

    1 cup uncooked white rice

    1 pkg. onion soup mix

    1 can cream of chicken soup

    1 can mushroom soup

    6 chicken breasts, frozen

    1 can water

Mix ingredients together, put into casserole dish, cover, and bake at 350° for 90 minutes.

RODEO RIBS

This is a favorite for my family and I serve it during the Ellensburg Rodeo.

Enough pork or beef ribs to feed the family
Barbecue sauce:

    1 cup ketchup

    1 Tbsp. Worcestershire sauce

    2-3 dashes bottled hot sauce

    1 cup water

    ¼ cup vinegar

    1 Tbsp. sugar

    1 tsp. salt

    1 tsp. celery seed

Prepare barbecue sauce by mixing all ingredients, then simmering for 30 minutes. Cut rack of ribs in serving pieces. Par-boil them for 20 minutes (important), and drain. When barbecue coals are gray, lower rack to lowest level possible. Put spareribs into sauce, then place them on the rack. Leave on the grill for seven minutes. Turn, baste with sauce and cook until ribs are brown and tender.

MEXI-CHILI CASSEROLE

1 lb. ground beef

1 8-oz. pkg. corn chips, crunched up

2 cups shredded cheddar cheese

1 15-oz. can chili with beans

1 15-oz. can enchilada sauce

1 8-oz. can tomato sauce

1 tsp. minced onion

1 cup sour cream

Preheat oven to 375°. Brown and drain ground beef. Reserve 1 cup corn chips and 1 cup cheese. Combine other chips, cheese, beef, chili, tomato sauce, enchilada sauce and onions. Pour mixture into casserole dish. Bake uncovered for 20 minutes or until heated through. Spread top with sour cream, sprinkle with remaining cheese, and make a ring around the edge of the casserole with corn chips. Bake five minutes longer. Makes six large servings.

BROCCOLI CASSEROLE

My niece, Debbie, shared this recipe with our family.

2 pkgs. frozen chopped broccoli

1 can cream of mushroom soup

1 cup mayonnaise

2 tsp. chopped onion

1 cup grated mild cheddar cheese

1 small can chopped water chestnuts

1 stack crackers

Put broccoli and onion into saucepan and cover with water. Bring to boil and cook for five minutes. Drain. Mix mayonnaise, water chestnuts and soup into drained broccoli and onions. Pour mixture into baking dish and bake at 350° for 30 minutes. Take out and stir in cheese, crumble the crackers on top, and return to oven for five minutes.

SAUSAGE AND EGG CASSEROLE

My daughter, Lori, serves this casserole on Christmas morning.

1½ lb. browned sausage

4 eggs

3 cups milk

1 can sliced mushrooms

1 can cream of mushroom soup

¾ tsp. dry mustard

2 cups grated cheddar cheese

8 slices bread, cubed or torn

Grease oblong baking dish. Place ingredients in layers: first layer – bread; second layer – sausage; third layer – mushrooms and cheese; fourth layer – mix 2½ cups milk with eggs and mustard. Cover and refrigerate at least three hours or overnight. Preheat oven to 300°. Mix ½ cup milk with soup and pour over top of casserole. Bake uncovered for 90 minutes. Enjoy!

CHINESE ALMOND CASSEROLE

Thanks to Linda Dozier.

Brown:

2 lbs. lean pork sausage

3 cups diced celery

2 chopped onions

1½ minced green peppers

1 small can pimentos

1½ cup raw rice

Boil according to directions:

4 single packages of dry chicken noodle soup

Add soup mixture to browned mixture. Stir in ¾ cup slivered almonds. Cover well in a casserole dish and bake 1 hour at 300 degrees. Uncover, if dry, add 1 cup water. Bake for 40 minutes more. Serves 16 to 18.

47

JANIS

My favorite recipe, "Buckaroo Potatoes" is a family favorite and tradition. They are especially good cooked over a campfire in a Dutch oven. Mother or Dad cooked "Buckaroo Potatoes" at home or when we stayed at Pete's Valley in our buckaroo camp. They sure tasted good after riding the range all day on my horse.

BUCKAROO POTATOES

Put a little oil in a Dutch oven. Add chopped bacon, onions, garlic, green peppers, sliced potatoes. Salt and pepper to taste. Cover and cook until done...stir occasionally and add a little water. Very good with beef or deer steak. There are no specific quantities, just peel potatoes and add the other ingredients according to the amount of folks you are serving.

Mother's Dutch oven still smells like "Buckaroo Potatoes". I use it a lot and savor the memories of family and buckaroo camp. Thanks Mother and Dad. It was fun being your little cowgirl. I loved our western life. Gosh! I could eat some of your "Buckaroo Potatoes" right now.

CALICO BEAN CASSEROLE

I always serve these beans over rodeo weekend and the cowpokes love them—thanks to dear Rita Hutchinson.

 1 lb. ground beef

 1 lb. lean bacon, chopped

 1 onion, chopped

 1 cup ketchup

 ½ cup barbecue sauce

 4 Tbsp. prepared mustard

 4 Tbsp. molasses

 1 tsp. chili pepper

 ¾ tsp. pepper   1 tsp. salt

 2 1-lb. cans red kidney beans

 2 1-lb. cans pork and beans

 2 1-lb. cans butter beans

Brown ground beef, bacon and onion. Drain. Combine meat with the rest of the ingredients, except the beans. Stir well, then add beans, including the juice. Bake for one hour at 350°. Makes 20-24 servings.

POTATO CASSEROLE

Joanne, my sister, gave me this outstanding recipe and now it is a family favorite!

 8 oz. sour cream

 1 can cream of chicken soup

 1 stick margarine

 2 bags frozen hash brown potatoes

 1 cup shredded cheddar cheese

 8 green onions, sliced

 1 cup corn flakes

 ¼ cup margarine

Mix sour cream, soup and stick of margarine (melted). Add potatoes, cheese, onions, salt and pepper to taste and mix well. Place in 9x13 buttered pan. Melt ¼ cup margarine and mix with corn flakes until coated. Spread corn flake mix over potatoes. Bake at 325° for one hour.

49

REFRIGERATOR ROLLS

Thanks to Jody Evitts. She has served lots of these delicious rolls to my family.

2 cups luke warm water

¾ cup sugar

1½ tsp. salt

2 pkgs. yeast, softened (This means that before you start mixing any of this up, put the yeast in about a half cup of luke warm water to let it start working.)

1 egg

¼ cu soft shortening

6 ½ to 7½ cups flour

Be sure the water is luke warm. One of the biggest mistakes with bread making is getting the water too hot. It should be about the temperature of a baby's bottle or when you put your hand in it is just slightly warmer than your body temperature. Mix all

ingredients, except flour, together in a big bowl. I usually put the shortening in the microwave and melt it, then add it first to the water. Add flour. The dough will be sticky. Mix it well, but you won't be able to knead it. Cover with a wet cloth in a greased towel and put it in the refrigerator overnight. In the morning, let rise until doubled, usually about 4 hours. Make into rolls about 1½ inches in diameter and place them in greased pan about one inch apart. Bake at 375° for 12 to 15 minutes. Makes about 3½ dozen rolls. I almost always double this recipe...they are so good and you can always put extras in the freezer.

50

POTATO DOUGHNUTS

Thank you, Gussie Dole, Jill McDowell's grandmother.

- **1 cup mashed potatoes**
- **1 cup sugar**
- **2 tbsp. melted shortening**
- **2 eggs, well beaten**
- **1 tsp. vanilla flavoring**
- **1 cup sifted flour**
- **½ cup evaporated milk**
- **½ cup water**
- **½ tsp. salt**
- **4 tsp. baking powder**
- **½ tsp. nutmeg**
- **Some extra flour, cinnamon and sugar.**

Combine mashed potatoes, sugar, shortening, eggs, milk, water and flavoring. Sift flour with salt, baking powder and nutmeg. Mix thoroughly and add sufficient flour to make a soft dough. Turn onto lightly floured board. Roll into a sheet ¼-inch thick and cut with floured doughnut cutter. Deep fry in oil at 365° for about two minutes or until well-browned. Drain on crumpled, absorbent paper and then roll in cinnamon-sugar mixture while still warm. Makes 40-45 servings.

CUSTARD

My mother baked a lot of custard as Dad, the haying crew, and I loved it.

- **4 eggs**
- **1 cup sugar**
- **1 tsp. salt**   **3 cups milk**
- **1 tsp. vanilla**

Beat eggs well in a mixing bowl, add sugar, milk, salt and vanilla – mix well. Bake at about 350° in round pan placed in a pan of water until a tan crust forms on top. A knife put through the custard will come out clean when it is done.

51

COCOA ROLL

In memory of my mother, Dorothy Capezzoli. Mother was a wonderful cook, and she always made this dessert for our family for a special treat. It is delicious.

5 eggs, separated

¾ cup sugar

¼ tsp. baking powder

2 heaping Tbsp. cocoa

1 tsp. vanilla

1 level Tbsp. flour

Separate eggs and beat yolks until lemon color (about 15 minutes) and beat whites until stiff. To the yolks add sugar and then flour, baking powder, chocolate, and vanilla. Fold in egg whites. Bake in flat pan at 375° for 15 minutes in the oven, then turn on a damp cloth to cool. Fill with whip cream, then roll up the cake and frost with chocolate frosting. Serve sliced one-inch thick.

SAUCES, SYRUPS & TOPPERS FOR YOUR TASTEBUDS

GRANDPA JERRY'S SYRUP

1 cup water

1 box light brown sugar

Bring water to boil. Slowly stir in sugar and remove pan from stove when sugar is dissolved. Enjoy on pancakes or biscuits.

HONEY BUTTER

My Aunt Virginia shared this recipe with me and it is yummy good!

½ cup honey

½ cup butter or margarine

½ tsp. cinnamon

1 cup powdered sugar

Beat all ingredients well with mixer and enjoy on biscuits or toast.

BUTTERED RUM MIX

My husband, Jerry, got me started on this recipe. It's nice to have on hand in the winter!

- ½ gallon ice cream
- 1 lb. brown sugar
- 1 lb. butter or margarine
- Rum

Mix ingredients (except rum), then put into the freezer to use as needed. Place frozen mix and rum in a mug of hot water and enjoy. Portion of mix and rum to be determined by choice.

HOT CHOCOLATE MIX

A cowboy friend from Oregon shared this recipe with my family. It is a wonderful mix to have on hand.

- 8 quart box instant dry milk
- 1 1-lb. box instant chocolate
- 1½ cup powdered sugar
- 1 6-oz. jar Coffee Mate

Mix all ingredients together and store in large container. Use about ¼ or ⅓ cup mix to 1 cup hot water.

Janis has two children and four grandchildren.

53

JANIS

IN A HURRY, LET'S DO IT THE EASY WAY

EASY INDIAN FRY BREAD

My cowpokes love fried bread and it is easy to serve. A cowgirl friend from Nevada gave our family the idea during the Ellensburg Rodeo. We are all grateful.

Make bread dough or purchase frozen bread dough in loaf form. The loaves are bagged and can be found in the freezer section. Use two loaves for small family and five for a larger family. Put frozen dough loaves in a covered container to rise, overnight is okay. To cook, break off small pieces of dough, pull or flatten and fry in hot oil until golden. Butter and enjoy topped with cinnamon sugar, powdered sugar, honey or jam.

TACO SOUP

   3 lbs. hamburger

   green pepper   onion

   4 large cans of tomatoes, undrained

   2 cans corn, undrained

   3 cans beans in any combination, undrained

   3 packages taco seasoning

Brown hamburger with green pepper and onion. Combine all ingredients and heat until bubbly. Serve with garnishes of your choice.

MUD MINT PIE

My girls fix this when I visit.

   chocolate syrup

   1 bag Oreo cookies, crushed

   ½ gallon mint chocolate chip ice cream

Put half the cookies on bottom of 9x13 pan. Drizzle melted butter on top. Add ice cream and put rest of cookies on top. Freeze. Drizzle with chocolate syrup before serving.

54

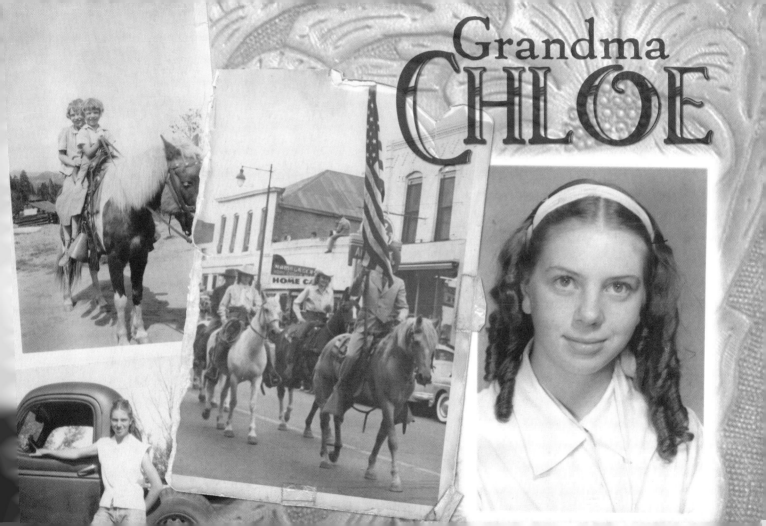

Grandma CHLOE

As the daughter of Lorraine Plass, Chloe Weidenbach, learned about ranch life at an early age. On her way to becoming an all-around roper, she got her first pony when she was 4 years old, and, as a teenager, served as the Rodeo Queen for the Adams County Fair and Rodeo in Colorado. Chloe and her husband Eldon currently have a beef cattle ranch on 480 acres of irrigated pasture. They hold weekly roping practice, and cow cutting and cow penning competitions in their indoor and outdoor arenas. The Weidenbachs are calf roping stock contractors for the Pacific Northwest, and train calf roping horses as well. Chloe, now 65, loves to share her ranch life with her four children and nine grandchildren.

SWEDISH MEAT BALLS

⅔ lb. ground round steak

⅓ lb. ground pork steak

1 egg, beaten

⅓ cup mashed potatoes

1 cup dry bread crumbs

⅓ tsp. brown sugar   2 tsp. salt

Scant ½ tsp each: black pepper, ginger, nutmeg, cloves, and allspice

⅓ cup milk   ⅔ cup cream

Mix all together to make a soft mixture that can barely be handled. Form into small balls and roll in flour. Fry on all sides in a small amount of hot fat until brown. Pour cream over the browned balls. Cover and let simmer slowly until the meat is very tender, about 30 minutes. Mixture may also be covered and placed in a slow oven for 40 minutes. Makes twelve 1¼" meatballs, very good warmed over.

SWEET & SOUR MEATBALLS

2 lbs. ground beef

¼ cup oatmeal

salt and pepper

1 egg   1 tsp. water

Mix above ingredients together and roll into balls. Roll in flour and brown, draining off any fat. Make the sauce..

1 can pineapple   2 Tbsp. soy sauce

¼ cup vinegar

¼ cup brown sugar

2 Tbsp. cornstarch

2 green peppers

Drain pineapple and reserve juice. Add water to make one cup liquid. Mix this with other ingredients and cook until thickened. Pour over meatballs and heat through.

57

FRUITS, VEGGIES & OTHER RANGE SALADS

SOUPS, CHILIES & OTHER POTS ON THE FIRE

COLESLAW

1 medium cabbage, chopped

1 tsp. salt

1 carrot, grated

½ green pepper, chopped

1 cup vinegar   ¼ cup water

1 tsp. mustard seed

1 tsp. celery seed   2 cups sugar

Mix cabbage and salt. Let stand one hour. Squeeze out moisture. Add carrots and peppers. Mix remaining ingredients for dressing and bring to boil for 1 minute. Cool until lukewarm. Pour over slaw and mix well. Pack into freezer containers, cover and freeze. This salad thaws quickly and remaining coleslaw may be refrozen The cabbage remains crisp.

CHLOE'S CHILI

5 lbs. pinto beans

salt and pepper

onion salt to taste

15 lbs. hamburger

3 Tbsp. chili powder

ketchup - just under a quart

onions to taste - chopped

1 large jar salsa

vinegar

Cover the pinto beans with water and soak for 24 hours or more. The longer you soak the beans, the bigger they get. Discard the soaking water and put beans into an electric roaster and add enough water to cover them. Add salt and pepper to taste. Cook the beans for 4 to 5 hours. Brown the hamburger, drain and add to the

58

beans. Add chili powder, onions, and ketchup (if you don't want your chili so sweet, add tomato sauce instead.) Just before serving, add the salsa. When serving, dollop a little vinegar on each serving of chili. Serves 55 to 75.

MEATS, CASSEROLES & OTHER COWPOKE VITTLES

HOMEMADE CORNED BEEF

5 lb. brisket (optional - tongue or heart)

1½ cup coarse salt

½ oz. saltpeter

1 Tbsp. brown sugar

9 bay leaves, crumbled, divided

2 Tbsp. pickling spice

8 cloves garlic, divided

1 onion, diced

½ cup vinegar

Combine 4 quarts of water, salt, saltpeter, brown sugar, six bay leaves and pickling spice. Boil 5 minutes, then cool. Place beef in large glass or stoneware crock. Add boiled mixture and 6 cloves garlic, slivered. Add extra water if needed to cover meat completely. Place heavy plate over meat, and add weight to keep meat submerged. Tie a piece of muslin over top of crock. Muslin should be taught and tied tightly. Cover crock, leaving a gap to allow some air circulation. Let crock stand in cool place 2 weeks.

At the end of 2 weeks, rinse meat well and place in dutch oven. Add fresh water to one inch above meat. Add 3 bay leaves, 2 garlic cloves, chopped garlic, one onion and vinegar. Bring to a boil, reduce heat and simmer until meat is tender, about 2 ½ to 3 hours. Allow meat to stand covered 30 minutes. Drain well. Trim off fat and thinly slice meat. If using tongue, peel off outside cover. Tongue makes good lunch meat. (For a different recipe, see the "easy way" section.)

59

CHOP SUEY

1 Tbsp. oil

1 lb. round steak, diced

½ lb. lean pork, diced

½ lb. lean veal, diced

salt & pepper

2 large onions, diced

2 Tbsp. soy sauce

1 bunch celery, diced

butter

1 cup Chinese vegetables

1 cup bean sprouts

Heat pressure cooker. Add fat and brown meat. Season with salt and pepper, onions, soy sauce. Place cover on cooker. Allow steam to flow from vent pipe to release all air from cooker. Place weight on meat and cook 10 minutes. After cooked and steam is released, remove lid, add drained vegetables and celery to meat. Heat in open cooker. Serve with steamed rice and/or Chinese noodles.

TACO CASSEROLE

1 lb. ground beef

2 cans chili

1 cup sliced black olives

l can salsa

l2 oz. cheddar cheese, grated or thinly sliced

1 cup crumbled taco chips

Brown hamburger and add chili, olives, and salsa and heat thoroughly. In the bottom of a casserole dish, put a layer of crumbled taco chips. Add a layer of the meat mixture and a layer of cheese. Repeat layers as many times as needed to use up meat mixture ending with cheese. Bake at 350° for 30 to 45 minutes or until cheese is melted. Decorate with additional chips and black olives.

SEAFOOD CASSEROLE

I really don't know where this recipe came from. I made it for a neighbor get-together.

1 can crab   1 can tuna

1 can shrimp, drained

1 cup celery, chopped

1 cup mayonnaise

1 can mushroom soup

1 Tbsp. minced onion

1½ cups milk

1 tsp. seasoning salt

1½ cups minute rice, cooked

4 hard boiled eggs, diced

1 Tbsp. ground pepper (optional)

grated or sliced cheese

Spread rice on the bottom and up sides of 9x13 casserole dish. Mix other ingredients together and spread on rice. Sprinkle with a light layer of cheese (I just lay individual slices of American cheese over the top.) Bake at 350° for 30 minutes or until cheese melts.

BEANS, POTATOES & OTHER SIDES FOR THE SADDLEBAG

BAKED BEANS

1 qt. dry beans (I use pinto)

1 lb. of pork, ham or bacon, chopped into pieces

1 medium onion, chopped

⅓ cup molasses   ¼ cup ketchup

1 tsp. salt   ⅓ tsp. pepper

½ tsp. dry mustard

2 Tbsp. brown sugar

Soak the beans overnight in cold water, drain and discard the liquid. Simmer in water for 2 to 3 hours. Drain and reserve liquid. Add beans, pork and onions into a 2-quart dish in layers. Mix remaining ingredients and pour over beans. Cover beans with reserved liquid and bake at 300° for 30 minutes.

61

CATTLEWOMEN'S BAKED BEANS

9 lbs. beans (I use pinto beans)

1 gallon water

½ cup salt

1¼ cups molasses

1¼ cups brown sugar

¼ cup dry mustard

4 to 4½ cups ketchup

3 quarts bean broth

2 onions chopped or 1 cup dry onion flakes

2 lbs. ham or bacon

½ cup more salt

Soak beans for approximately 24 hours. Drain and add more water and salt. Cover and simmer until tender, approximately one day. Drain and reserve bean broth. Add remaining ingredients, including three quarts bean broth. Cover and bake at 375° in an electric roaster for 6 to7 hours. One half hour before serving, remove lid and finish cooking. To keep the beans from sticking, put water under the tray in the electric roaster and stir beans periodically. Serves 50 –75

A spray or two of apple cider vinegar (do not dilute) on the top of bean type dishes, such as, baked beans, chili, or bean soups when served, eliminates the poppers! I keep a spray bottle handy at all times.

BREADS, DESSERTS & OTHER SWEETS FROM THE RANGE

CORNBREAD

I made this and the baked bean recipe on page 61 with Forence Henderson on NBC's "Today" show.

2 eggs	2 cups buttermilk
1 tsp. soda	¼ cup sugar
1 tsp. baking powder	
¼ cup flour	2 cups corn meal
3 Tbsp. vegetable oil	

Mix ingredients, pour batter into a greased 9x13 pan. Bake at 400° for 25 minutes.

BAKING POWDER BISCUITS

2 cups flour	l tsp. salt
3 tsp. baking powder	
6 Tbsp. shortening	
⅔ cup milk	

Sift together dry ingredients. Cut in shortening and add milk. Round up on a floured board. Knead lightly and roll out or pat to ½ inch thick. Cut into biscuits and place on an ungreased baking sheet. Bake to golden brown at 400° for l5 minutes.

My first loaf of bread was a flop. The recipe said to scald the milk...I did and added it and finished the recipe even though it did not raise...I put it in a bread pan and baked it and then threw it out. Our dog found it and buried it, even he wouldn't eat it!

HOT ROLLS

My mother-in-law is the best cook and this is her recipe. When I was a new bride, she helped me become the cook I am.

3 pkgs. dry yeast, dissolved in ½ cup warm water.

3 Tbsp. sugar

⅔ cup milk   1½ tsp. salt

½ cup sugar   6 Tbsp. butter

3 eggs

4 cups sifted flour (plus a little extra)

Add sugar to yeast and let stand. If it bubbles yeast is good. In a sauce pan put milk, salt, sugar, butter. Warm and mix together. Beat eggs and add to yeast mixture. Stir in flour. Sift more flour on board for kneading dough. Keep it a little sticky but still be able to handle. Put in a greased bowl and cover. Let stand in a warm place 1½ hours. Punch down and let raise another ½ hour.

Arrange dough however you like. Bake at 350° for 20 or more minutes until light brown.

64

PECAN ROLLS (use hot roll recipe)

4 Tbsp. butter

1 cup brown sugar

½ cup corn syrup

½ to 1 cup chopped or whole pecans

2 Tbsp. melted butter

cinnamon

In bottom of a 9x13 pan, melt butter. Sprinkle with brown sugar. Add corn syrup (just dribble over brown sugar) and sprinkle with pecans. Roll out dough as for cinnamon rolls. Sprinkle with melted butter and cinnamon to taste. Cut about 1 to 1½ inches and roll. Place on pecan mixture and let rise. Bake at 350° for 20 to 25 minutes or till a little brown. Remove from oven and invert pan on a serving dish, platter, cookie sheet or another pan.

SOURDOUGH STARTER

This recipe came from my sister Betty Swisher, Badger Minnesota.

2 cups warm potato water

2 cups flour

1 Tbsp sugar

Mix till smooth paste. Put in warm place overnight till double.

SOURDOUGH HOTCAKES

2 cups starter

2 eggs

1 tsp salt

1 Tbsp sugar

1 tsp soda

2 Tbsp melted fat or oil

Mix together, bake on griddle.

SOURDOUGH BREAD

To ½ cup starter add 1 cup flour and 1 cup warm water and put away for next time.
To the rest of starter, add:

4 cups flour

1 tsp salt

2 Tbsp sugar

Sift flour, salt & sugar together into a bowl. Make a well in the middle. Pour starter into well & mix. Then add fat and mix well. Add ¼ tsp soda in 1 Tbsp warm water and mix in. Place in bowl, cover, and let rise till double in a warm place. Punch down, place in a greased loaf pan and let rise until double again. Bake 375* for 55 minutes.

65

JUNE'S BANANA BREAD

1 cup Crisco

4 eggs

1 ⅓ cup sugar

1 tsp. salt

5 large bananas

2 tsp. soda

3½ cups flour

1 cup nuts

Cream first four ingredients together. Puree bananas to make three cups of liquid and add to creamed mixture. Add soda, flour and nuts. Mix well and divide batter between two greased loaf pans. Bake at 300° for 75 minutes.

DOUGHNUTS

I bake for the ropers that come to our arena. This is just what they go for. It takes about 5 hours to complete.

½ cup warm water	2 pkg dry yeast
⅔ cup milk	½ cup sugar
1 tsp salt	½ cup butter
2 eggs	
4 –7 cups sifted flour	

Dissolve yeast in water. Put milk and sugar in a saucepan and heat through but not hot. Blend salt, butter, and eggs. Beat until mixed and add to yeast. Stir in four cups sifted flour and add another three cups if desired to knead. Knead for five minutes or so, but don't make dough dry. Place in greased dish and allow to rise for 90 minutes. Punch down and allow to rise another ½ hour. Roll out to 1 inch thick, cut into doughnuts and let rise on board until very light.

Heat grease to 375° and fry doughnuts until brown on both sides. Remove and ice with sugar.

CARROT CAKE

  3 cups ground or shredded carrots

  2 cups flour

  2 tsp. baking soda

  1 tsp. cinnamon

  ½ tsp. salt

  2 cups sugar

  1 cup ground or shredded coconut

  1 cup oil

  1 cup chopped nuts

  4 eggs

Beat eggs, add sugar and oil. Mix in dry ingredients. Add carrots, nuts and coconut. Bake at 350° for 30 to 45 minutes in a 9x13 pan. Top with frosting.

Frosting:

  1 cube butter

  1 pkg. powdered sugar

  1 large pkg. cream cheese

Beat together and spread on cooled cake.

RHUBARB CAKE

  2 cups flour

  1¼ cup sugar

  1 egg

  ½ cup shortening

  1 tsp. soda

  ¼ tsp. salt

  1 tsp. vanilla

  1 cup butter or sour milk

  2 cups sliced rhubarb

Topping:

  ½ cup sugar

  1 Tbsp. cinnamon

  1 Tbsp. butter

Combine cake ingredients, mixing well and adding rhubarb last. Fold into a greased 13x9x2 pan. Crumble mixture of topping ingredients over cake. Bake at 350° for 35-40 min. Serves 12.

67

NUT CAKE

Thank you to Mrs. Wallace for this one.

- 2¼ cup sugar
- ¾ cup butter
- 3 tsp. baking powder
- 3 cups flour
- 1½ cup nut meats coarsely chopped
- 1½ cup sweet milk
- 6 egg whites beaten stiff and fold in

Cream together sugar and butter. Sift baking powder and flour and add to mixture. Blend in nut meats, milk and egg whites. Bake 30 minutes at 350° and 20 minutes at 375°. Top with icing.

Icing:

- 1½ cup brown sugar
- 1½ cup sweet cream
- 1 tsp. vanilla
- Boil sugar and cream until thick. Flavor with vanilla and spread over cake.

GRANDPA HENRY'S CHOCOLATE CAKE

- 3 cups flour
- ¾ cup cocoa
- 2 cups sugar
- 1 tsp. baking powder
- 2 tsp. soda
- 2 Tbsp. vinegar
- 2 tsp. vanilla
- ¾ cup oil
- 2 cups water

Mix in 9x13 pan and bake at 350° for about 45 minutes or until done.

ANNA'S MOLASSES CAKE

1 egg, beaten

½ cup sugar

2 Tbsp. butter, melted

3 cups flour

2 tsp. baking soda

¾ cup molasses

2 cups hot water

Mix all ingredients and bake in a 9 x 13 pan and bake at 350° for about 45 minutes.

PIE CRUST

A good Cattlewomen recipe. Thank you Barbara Weber.

3 cups flour	1 tsp. salt
1 cup Crisco	1 Tbsp. vinegar
6 Tbsp. cold water	1 egg, beaten

Sift together flour and salt. Cut in Crisco and add vinegar, water and egg.

COBBLER

1 cup sugar

1 cup flour

pinch of salt

4 tsp. baking powder

2 Tbsp. melted butter

1 cup milk

4 or 5 cups fruit

1 cup sugar

2 cups hot water

Mix sugar, flour, salt, baking powder, butter and milk in order and pour into greased baking dish. Bring to boil fruit, sugar and water and pour over dough. Bake at 350° about 30 minutes.

69

ICE CREAM

2 cups milk

½ tsp. salt

2½ cups sugar

½ cup plus 2 Tbsp. flour

8 eggs

6 cups whipping cream

Heat milk in a saucepan with salt, sugar and flour. Heat until thick, stirring constantly, about 15 minutes. Beat the eggs until smooth and add some of the hot mixture. Mix well and add the rest of the hot mixture. Refrigerate for two hours or more. Add the whipping cream and then follow the instructions of your ice cream maker. See hot fudge sauce for topping.

SAUCES, SYRUPS & OTHER TOPPERS FOR YOUR TASTEBUDS

BEEF MARINADE

1 cup Worcestershire sauce

¼ to ½ cup soy sauce

couple drops of Tabasco sauce

1 C butter or margarine

Heat ingredients to boiling, pour immediately over beef. Marinade for 5 to 6 hours, turning every 2 hours. Also, good to marinade hamburger patties.

TEXAS BARBECUE SAUCE

2 tsp. brown sugar

1 Tbsp. paprika

1 tsp. salt

1 tsp. dry mustard

¼ tsp. chili powder

⅛ tsp. cayenne pepper

¼ cup vinegar

1 cup tomato juice

¼ cup ketchup

½ cup water

Mix ingredients in a saucepan and simmer for 15 minutes or until slightly thickened.

CHLOE'S FROSTING

3 Tbsp. flour

1 cup milk

½ cup butter

½ cup oil

⅛ tsp. salt

1 cup granulated sugar

flavoring and coloring (optional)

Heat flour and milk while stirring until thick, then cool. At room temperature, add butter, oil and salt. Beat until thick and high. Then add sugar, flavoring and coloring.

Chloe has four children and nine grandchildren.

71

HOT FUDGE SAUCE

2 to 4 squares unsweetened baking chocolate

1 cup butter or margarine

3 cups sugar

1 large can evaporated milk

In a double boiler, melt chocolate and butter. Add sugar (½ cup at a time) and mix well. It will get real stiff. In small portions, stirring after each, add evaporated milk. Keep beating until sugar is dissolved. Serve warm and add vanilla if desired.

IN A HURRY, LET'S DO IT THE EASY WAY

MEAT LOAF

This is a real quick way to go if you are busy. You can slice and use for sandwiches. If you like it sweet use ketchup or chili sauce.

1 lb. ground beef

½ cup quick oatmeal

1 egg

salt

pepper

onion

6-oz. can tomato paste

Mix beef with oatmeal and add salt, pepper, and onion to taste. Blend. Add half can of tomato paste and mix with hands or spoon. Put in a loaf pan and spread with remaining tomato paste. Bake at 350° to 400° for one hour.

"EASY WAY" CORNED BEEF

2 lb beef chuck or short ribs

1 onion

2 cloves garlic

4 peppercorns

2 stalks celery

2 cans condensed consomme

Place meat in pressure cooker. Add all ingredients and two cans water. Cook at 10 lbs pressure for 20 minutes. Let stand for pressure to loosen lid. It's great and could not be more tender. (If you've got more time between cattle drives, see "Homemade Corned Beef" in Grandma Chloe's section.)

BOILED STEW

You can use chuck, soup bone, neck bone or what is left in your freezer. Boil until done for about two to three hours. Let cool over night. Take off all fat and bones. Shred meat in the broth. Add potatoes and any vegetables that are handy. Onion, carrots, peas, green beans, corn, cabbage, tomatoes. It all cooks together. Cook till vegetables are done. Its great on the trail.

QUICK HOT FUDGE SAUCE

2 squares unsweetened baking chocolate

½ cube butter

1 can sweetened condensed milk

In a double boiler, heat all ingredients until melted.

73

INDEX BY CATEGORY

Dips, Mixes & Other Stuff For Grazin'

Guacamole Dip 41
Jalapeno Tortilla Rolls 41
Jill's Party Mix 3
Seven Layer Bean Dip 21
Swedish Meat Balls 57
Sweet & Sour Meatballs 57

Fruits, Veggies & Other Range Salads

Coleslaw 58
Cucumbers In Sour Cream 23
Fruit Salad 22
Hazel's Cranberry Salad 42
Ice Box Pickles 21
Yummy Salad 22

Soups, chilies & other pots on the fire

Chloe's Chili 58
Cream Of Potato Soup 4
Dumpling Recipe For Stew Or Chicken 4
Hamburger Stew 23
Southwest White Chili 43
Texas Beef Chili 44

Meats, Casseroles & Other Cowpoke Vittles

Baked Salmon 8
Beef & Vegetable Casserole 7
Beef Noodle Bake 7
Broccoli Casserole 46
Chelsy's Lazy Day Lasagna 26
Chicken & Biscuits 6
Chicken & Elbow-roni 6
Chicken Casserole 45
Chinese Almond Casserole 47
Chop Suey 60
Golden Meat Loaf 5
Hamburger Corn Bake 25
Homemade Corned Beef 59
Kraut Pot Pie 6
Lasagna Presto 8
Mexi-chili Casserole 46
Rodeo Ribs 45
Salmon Loaf 24
Sausage And Egg Casserole 47
Seafood Casserole 61
Stroganoff 25

74

Sweet And Sour Pork 5
Taco Casserole 60
Vegetable Loaf 24

Beans, Potatoes & Other Sides For The Saddlebag

Baked Beans 61
Buckaroo Potatoes 48
Calico Bean Casserole 49
Cattlewomen's Baked Beans 62
Cheesy Potato Bake 28
Grandpa's Poker Beans 9
Potato Casserole 49
Twice-baked Potatoes 27

Breads, Desserts & Other Sweets From The Range

Anna's Molasses Cake 69
Apple Crisp 10
Apple Crisp 31
Apple Nut Cake 10
Baking Powder Biscuits 63
Carrot Cake 67
Chocolate Chip Pie 33
Choco-marshmallow Cookies 35
Cobbler 69

Cocoa Roll 52
Corn Cakes 12
Cornbread 63
Cowboy Cake 32
Crazy Cake 32
Custard 51
Doughnuts 66
Dream Bars 34
Grandpa Henry's Chocolate Cake 68
Holiday Carrot Pudding 28
Hot Rolls 64
Ice Cream 70
Impossible Pie 12
June's Banana Bread 66
Lacey's Monster Cookies 35
Mince Meat 14
Mom's Icing Or Fudge 33
Nut Cake 68
Old-fashioned Rice Pudding 14
Pecan Rolls 64
Peanut Butter Logs 13
Pie Crust 11
Pie Crust 69
Pie Crust Cookies 34
Plain Muffins 12
Potato Doughnuts 51
Potato Rolls 30
Sourdough Bread 65

75

Sourdough Hotcakes 65
Sourdough Starter 65
Rhubarb Cake 67
Rhubarb Crisp 11
Refrigerator Rolls 65
Texas Sheet Cake 30
Traditional English Cookie 13

Sauces, Syrups & Toppers For Your Tastebuds

Beef Marinade 70
Chloe's Frosting 71
Cocoa Frosting 36
Cream Cheese Spread 15
Grandpa Jerry's Syrup 52
Honey Butter 52
Hot Fudge Sauce 72
Texas Barbecue Sauce 71

Liquers, Cordials & Other Sippin' Stuff

Buttered Rum Mix 53
Cherry Cordial 16
Homemade Kahlua 16
Hot Chocolate Mix 53

In A Hurry, Let's Do It The Easy Way

Boiled Stew 73
Broccoli Casserole 38
Chocolate Fudge Cookies 36
Cinnamon Apple Toast 37
Easy Indian Fry Bread 54
"Easy Way" Corned Beef 73
Goulash 18
Meat Loaf 72
Mud Mint Pie 54
Mud Pie 37
One Dish Meal 18
Quick Hot Fudge Sauce 73
Six Cup Fruit Salad 38
Sloppy Joes 18
Spaghetti Pizza 17
Taco Soup 54
Tuna Fish Open-facers 17

Weights and Measures

3 teaspoons = 1 tablespoon

2 tablespoons = 1 liquid ounce

4 tablespoons = ¼ cup

5 ⅓ tablespoons = ⅓ cup

16 tablespoons = 1 cup

1 cup = 8 ounces

2 cups = 1 pint

4 cups = 1 quart

2 tablespoons fat = 1 ounce

½ pound butter or fat = 1 cup

1 pound granulated sugar = 2 cups

1 pound brown sugar = 3 cups

1 pound confectioners sugar = 3½ cups

1 pound flour = about 4 cups

1 pound rice = 2 cups

1 pound cheese = 5 cups, grated

1 package cream cheese = 3 ounces or 6 Tbs.

1 cup chopped nutmeats = ¼ pound

16 marshmallows = ¼ pound

½ pint heavy cream = 1 cup, whipped

Grandma Lorraine preparing her laripin' good Rubber Chicken Stew.